HEARTHSTON

£2.99

Joseph Butler

Two Rivers Press

*With thanks to: Jenny Lewis, Olly Mantell,
Bruno Guastalla, Keiren Phelan, Steven Egan,
John & Caroline Pickering, Wyon Stansfeld,
John & Lady Juliet Townsend*

First published in the UK in 2006 by
Two Rivers Press
35–39 London Street
Reading RG1 4PS
www.tworiverspress.com

Book and cover design by Sally Castle

Printed and bound by Conservatree
Print and Design Ltd, Reading

ISBN 1-901677-43-5
978-1-901677-43-0

Contents

These pages are dedicated to my father; and to the memory of Wilfred Grant, blacksmith in Charlton village (b 1908, d 1994).

Hera

He was to have been a gift
to my seeker-after-trifles,
to the glad-eyed lord-and-master
in whose loving I once shone:
a son to curb his wandering,
a baby boy to still his lust;
when all he craved was conquest and the chase.

So maybe he was ill-starred from the start.
Maybe it was hope that skewed his shaping.
But all those months of pregnancy I dared to dream;
grew fat with dreaming, full of it.
I came to term and squatted, sweated,
thrust him out – my talisman,
the being who'd absorbed me for so long.

And nothing about him was lovely,
beyond his being there at all.
Behind my head I heard
the midwives hiss and sputter.
They swaddled him against my prying fingers,
hid their news from me and fled.

He'll tell you that I never loved him
but that's not true. It's just
that my dream was lithe, and fleet-of-foot,
a-caper in the span
between his father and myself;
just that dreaming died
in the jumble of bone beneath his waist –
that he did not fit his purpose.

And we lived then in a crueller age –
the old, infirm, the very young
pegged out on hillsides
for lions or the snows to take.
So I carried him
to the margins of our heaven.
I held him for a while,
a very little while,
and threw him off.

Forgework

I

In the fire the atoms quicken
in their dance. Steel
reinvents itself, assumes
the colour of coals,
is leavened, livid, quick with heat.
I take it from the hearth
and its glow casts shadows,
a wakefulness beneath my hands.
And each blow counts,
each hammer-stroke is eloquent
to lengthen and compress,
to curve and flare and curl,
for what was base is golden
only for an instant.
And metal blues and stiffens,
grows sullen underneath the hammer's face.
Is master of itself once more.

2

In his rages nowhere was safe.
He was fist and spittle,
loveless, unrelenting.
His anger seeped through walls,
crushed thought, laid childhood bare.
I listened from my bedroom
as his fury pocked and rammed
my mother's flesh.
I watched her in the morning
nurse muesli past a broken lip.
She hid her arms
and buttoned blouses at the neck.
In the sudden silence of his leaving
we sobbed.

3

Between the hammer and the anvil
metal shimmers, the flames' fruit
pares to ribbons
that bear the hammer's blows,
grow shapely.
I loop their knotwork keep-safes
over gates and screens; spin out a tracery
on balustrades and arches.
On empty air steel dances,
and in the rhythm of the hammer's blows
I feel my own resistance shaken.
My anger scales away.
I'm weightless, joyful,
scarred and dancing,
hurt remade.

Ammonite

As a child I watched
the peel and splinter of slate
as you picked in the cliff face
for fossils.

Something beautiful about the coils
that you dislodged, their corrugations
clenched across millennia,
stranded in a sea-bed turned to rock
that reared above the crust we stood on.

Something fantastical, even then,
about the sense you made of time,
the gaps it spanned
and their inversion
of the solid and the liquid things.

And something precious in that shore
whose gold grain ran a thread
between the old sea and the new,
the stone sea and the wind-ruffed
restless charge of water-onto-land.

You lent me your hammer to play with.
Its weight in my hand, the swing of it
too large, its bounce and skew discarded,
abandoned on a rock.

Back at the car your anger rushed like water,
gathered the horizon to itself and took me,
rolled me over, spun the world –
left me battered, breathless, still as stone.

And I remember how you ran,
with no thought but the hammer,
back across the beach to beat the tide,
your footsteps flailing in the sand.

Smelting

That year you rented rooms
that overlooked the sweep of Swansea Bay –
the steelworks at Port Talbot spread below
like a scumline on the shore.
Your speech unstiffened, and behind your eyes
there glowed the memory of rock
at temperatures so high
it moved as liquid.

You looked down onto poisoned land –
the maze of railway sidings, pipework,
the mile-long run of rolling-sheds.
And cragged above the rest the furnaces:
those fanned, fantastic crucibles
in whose inferno-heart the ore unmade itself,
gave up its prize; where steel ran weeping
from the sloughed husk of its skin.

By day you studied slag, pored over
cooled and vitreous remains
of what had once been lodestone.
You analysed the marriage made of burning rock.
And in the evenings you painted,
played oils across a nightscape:
the flare-stack and those flame-drenched roofs
stark against translucent sea.

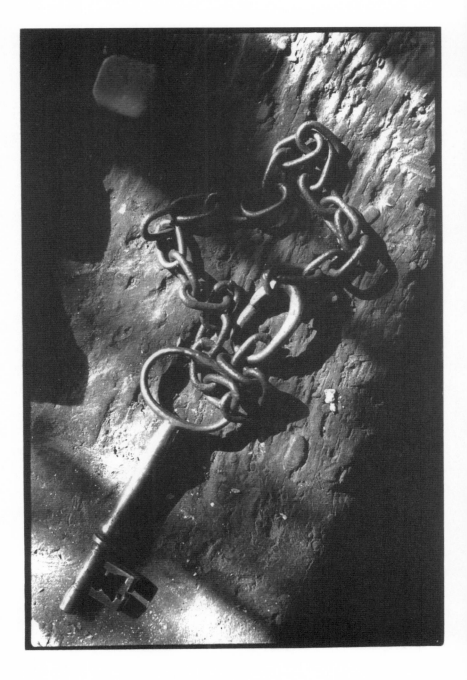

Opening up

Even the key was his work,
the bow brazed to the stock,
the wards hand-filed and riveted
so not-quite-perfectly, so hair's breadth loose
you had to fish in the deadlock
for the leverage that slipped the bolt.

And the sense, in the lift of the latch
and the scuff of the timbers over the kerb,
of breaking a seal.
The forge unstoppered: a tarry antiseptic breath
of woodsmoke and extinguished coals,
taste of steel like blood in the nostrils,
the seep of damp through undressed stone.

A clatter of daylight over the sill,
and the breath indrawn.
In the gloom the hunch of the hearth,
a crouch and a stillness of bellows –
folds roofed with dust, soused-supple with linseed.
Their pumping-handle,
ashwood grain palmed smooth with use,
cranes forward, considers.

The whole place appraising.
I feel myself weighed.
A judgement made, withheld, deferred.
And into it my own voice pitched,
a tremor in the air:
Have faith.
This is no trespass.

Football

After three years of beatings
my Mum grew indistinct,
was no less height nor breadth
but chipped and colourless and fading.
I didn't love her less
but loved more carefully,
afraid she'd pull me through her papery skin
to the place she'd gone to ground,
to the place that muffled sound
when he hit her.
In lulls in his anger I caught her eye.
I kicked a football, grazed my knees
and even as she bandaged me
I willed the thought:
flesh bruises, is resistant.

Thetis

I live with my sister in the summer-caves.
Reflected light of ocean whispers on the rocks.
We lie in each other's arms and look up at the light.
All my life it has been like this –
I honour what is changeful,
hold my balance while the world eddies round me.
I am the still point, the calm to which the sea returns
from wave and storm and umbrage.
My eyes are its blue, and cold and clear as ocean.
My thoughts break the surface like porpoise.

A boy came to us, an immortal.
We think that one day he will be a king.
He tells us that he fell from heaven
and we smile and soothe his babbling.
I put him to my breast and he sucks like a seal-pup.
He drains me and it is exquisite.
Milk spills and runs between my breasts,
it crusts on my belly, cracks as I stretch.
He coils his fingers in my hair and tugs.
The veins beat at his temples,
blue beneath his cap of hair.
His rage is monstrous, undeniable.
He beats into our stillness and slowly
his anger ceases. He is calm.

Kindling

Weigh the axe, and sight the blow.
Bring the hissing steel's edge down
to sever wood along its grain.
Repeat…

The wedged head cleaves a line
round which the growth of years divides.
The fibres of a summer's fullness
rend from one another.

Again…
The noise you hear a compound
of the bedding of the blow,
the shock and snap of wood's resistance.
And what's exposed is splintered, frayed –

the raggedness
on which the flame's edge
preys, seizes, claims its hold,
begins to work
its dissolution.

Gifthorse

It was a roadside happenstance,
a found poem: four stone walls
and a wooden lean-to,
the space behind it snagged
with bramble, dogrose.

Water seeped from a rain-butt,
furled damp around a grindstone.
Creepers choked the channels
of a corrugated roof.

I've never had the gift of trusting providence –
between my seeking and the finding
there've been gaps too full of chanciness.
So when the sought-for thing appears
I look at it askance.

Glass panes filmed like cataracts.
Through a fracture in the casement
you could see the rust-bloom on an anvil,
the cowling of a brick-built hearth.
And still I doubted; nosed the smithy
as a creature would a trap.

As though the bleached wood of the lintel
might buckle; chimney jolt
and render back to brick.
As though the mortar of the place
might leach away,
and those untenanted stones collapse.

Within the walls the bellows
at the fire's back sighed.

Hephaistos 1

They would have had me graze on shellfish.
They fed me with mussels and clams,
titbits of oysters, the sweet flesh of crabs.
They clothed me in rags of sailcloth and seaweed
and taught me to walk.

They showed me only tenderness,
lullabied me to the rhythms
of the suck and rush of tides.
"Listen," they said,
and held the conch shell to my ear.
"Listen, Hephaistos…"
But I had ears for something else.

In the rage at the world's core
the molten metal slops and seethes,
thrusts upwards through faultlines
to scar and scab the green.

In caves by the Aegean
I watched the fires that played across the water,
smelt the sulphur on the brine,
saw in their flickering something that was mine
and set myself to win it.

Over centuries I refined and purified,
drew riches out of rock, till in my hands I held
the essences of Tin, and Lead,
of Copper, Zinc and Iron,
prised unalloyed from lodestone.
And wrought in them
the slow, arrested, liquid shapes
of the element that broke my fall.

Tilth

For four nights by a hunter's moon
you worked the patch of ground
behind the forge. You hoed

the lines of cauliflowers and cabbages
whose plump hearts folded to themselves
the dewy darkness. You earthed

potato roots, plied water from the rain-butt
to the wigwam-frame of runner beans.
Their rustling shivered upwards

to the summer stars. Now couch grass
overruns the plot. I rake away
the bindweed and the bramble,

work the spade's edge down
between the nettles and the dock.
Beneath their roots the soil

is opalescent, finely tilled.
It's crumbed with horses' dung
and moonlight.

Jack-the-Lad

Cadger of fags, bad debtor,
borrower of fivers on the never-never,
he finger-combs the quiff across his thinning scalp,
sucks the froth off a pint,
squints down the scar-line that distorts his cheek.
The tale…?
A six-inch gap that opened in his face
that time he smacked his bike into the tarmac
on the bend above the hill…

Aged ten he's shinning up the wall
behind the forge, and cunning as a rat
treads out along the tiles towards the chimney-pot.
November. Bag of bangers in his pocket.
Below him he can hear the scuff of feet,
the scrape of steel on coals.
He sees the fire's glow
circled on the chimney's lip,
and tosses in the bag…

Louder than the bang the roar
the old man gave, erupting
like a badger baited from its lair,
hair a sweat-stiffed halo, fists like hams.
Jack skitters off the roof and runs.

Behind him, stride for stride, the smith
his apron flapping like a sail,
the starlit street grown deafening
to the slap and stamp of his pursuit.

Out onto open country, up the hill
past Rainsborough Camp they run,
the child half-spent and sobbing,

frit to death; the blacksmith's footfall
vivid with the sparks
his boots strike from the asphalt.
They skid and fade and die.
His breathing comes in gasps.

Orion wheels above them in the sky.
The child runs on, is lost to sight –
a flare and then a darkness in the Hunter's eye.

Wilfred

Mid-morning.
I glanced up from the fire
to the shock of his scrutiny:

his body hunkered in the doorway,
hunched and sparrow-slight,
his knuckles blue-ing on the upright of the frame.

He watched hungry as a boy,
but I felt my every movement weighed
against the stock of memory

his frame contained,
and knew myself clumsy, coltish,
the blows snatched, their aim misplaced.

Only when he'd gone
did the rhythm return:
cautious as a startled horse,

but workaday and powerful;
haltered in the compass of his vision,
in its reach and in its fading.

Physics

Maybe the physics then was simpler.
Or, if not the physics, then the physicality:
a world whose workings lay revealed,
its mechanisms open
to the probing and the remedy
of eye and hand.

So as you straightened out a plough-blade
your senses told you when the thing was true.
You could see the furrow that the steel would cut.

Even, at the end, the Morris Traveller
you parked inside the shoeing shed
was still just nuts and bolts
to take apart and reassemble.

And all the horses that you shod
so daintily: anatomies
of cartilage and bone
that jigged and fretted
to the leverage of ligament,
the tensioning of muscle;
connections there for you to figure out by touch
beneath the sweetly smelling, hay-encrusted skin.

The flex before the crafty bastard kicked.

Shoeing shed

That evening
I lit a candle in the shoeing shed,
in the place

he'd stooped and sweated,
lifted hooves
to brand the horn with slippery steel.

It burned all night,
puddled wax
in the channels of the cobbled floor.

It was summer
and the white froth of nettle
flowers craned in at the window;

columbine and vetch
trailed their stems
the length of the metal rack.

In the cemetery
the swallows skirled and feinted
through the cypress shelter-belt.

The clod I tossed into the grave
was warm, husked with sunlight.
It shattered on the coffin lid.

Triptych

1 Father

I don't remember the first time that I hit her.
I don't recall the impact of my knuckles on her cheek,
or the way her jaw sagged open. It's a blur
to me, the way we both went rigid with the shock,
and the way I kept on shouting, and how good
it felt, at last, to let it out, to stop pretending
I felt anything but love. How the blood
from her nose kept on dripping, and how she kept on
dabbing at it, telling me it didn't matter.
I don't remember stepping out of one place
into another, where the rules were suddenly different,
where the rules we'd always lived by weren't coherent
– just the mark of my hands on her face.
It takes all my effort. Still I don't remember.

2 *Mother*

As a child I sat in a boat that slipped its moorings,
and drifted in a dazzle of reflected light
away across the stillness of a loch.
And the point at which I took fright
came not with the sight of water lapping
through the boards, but was prompted by the voices
of my Aunt and Uncle shouting from a bank
that was suddenly, shockingly green,
each needle of the larches like a pinprick in my vision.
It's like that now, only it's as though
I've drifted out of earshot. I see the mouths
of those I'm closest to split open in a soundless "O",
as comical as fishes, as empty as the *moue* I make
to the lipsticked woman in the mirror.

3 Child

If I put this brick here, just like so
then Mummy will be safe, so I must be careful.
I'm building a house for us out of Lego.
It doesn't have a roof but, look, you pull
the door open and you can see us inside.
The carpet's green, and my Mum is in the kitchen.
Up the stairs is my room. I keep it tidy
so that Daddy won't be cross; and when I've finished
building
I'm going to read my book. I like my book,
it's sad, and maybe, when I've reached the end I'll cry.
I hate the noise that Mum and Dad make
when they fight. I lie in bed and listen
and the noises in the night sound like earthquakes
and volcanoes in my book about the Earth.

Upset

There's a point at which the grain reverses,
rucks and
crumples where it meets resistance:

the domed head of a rivet, say –
that plumpening
where you overturn the shank

and splay and peen
the upset
with the ball-end of the hammer.

Or the shoulder of a tenon where
what matters
is the meat in the bar:

you're striking down the upright length
towards the heat –
the soft end bluntens, a collision

into which the forged steel's forced,
shock waves
spilling outwards to expand its girth.

What's needed
is an impact
that's diffuse – the bar a ram

which each new blow concusses:
a node-point
forming where the steel has packed,

the skin around it puckered,
inexpressive,
taut as cicatrice, or chrysalis.

Sons

The sons of violent men find loving hard.
What your unreason taught me was to be afraid.
The love you call your loving leaves me scarred,

as frightened of your touch as of your disregard.
Devalued by the currency in which you trade
the sons of violent men find loving hard,

their gifts inadequate. I brand myself a coward
for not coming to my mother's aid –
the love you call your loving leaves me scarred

when others who I love end up disfigured,
when every act of loving is a love betrayed.
The sons of violent men find loving hard

until they find it in them to discard
this artless, heartless masquerade:
"The love you call your loving leaves me scarred,"

I say, "as, in your boyhood, you yourself were scarred."
Behind you there's another and another shade:
the sons who found their path to manhood barred.
The love that came before us leaves us scarred.

Wilfred Grant, *centre*, with father Frank, *left*, and
grandfather Samuel, *right* (photograph taken c1925)

Dead men

I am warded by dead men,
guided by ghosts;
their touch on my arm is deft,
I fear for the skill in my hands.

I take his tools down from the rack
and watch
as the scroll coils,
the steel draws down.
The drift sinks plumb-centre
through the body of the bar.

These things are gifted:
I step into their spell.

In the upswing of the hammer
the blow's intuition.
In the pressure of my knuckles on the tongs
a nicety of angles judged.
As though their palms had printed on the place
a knowledge-hoard
that's mine to touch.

And at its heart the fire,
the cave of coals
through which the bellows' pulsing soughs.
Behind the suck-and-push of leather
I hear the sibilance of heat
that spreads along the bar.
The looseness that precedes the burning,
the lucent dangerousness of steel,
the hiss of their companionship.

Grandfather

When he grew too old for forgework
your grandfather would sit on a canvas strap
slung between the uprights of his workbench
on the south wall of the smithy –

the hooks he hung it from remain,
embedded in the bench-legs
that straddle the vice

in whose jaws he'd clench
the wedged head of a horseshoe-nail
and, with a file, silver the tip
to the sharpness of a needle,

while you stood at the fire and fullered
the furrow in the shoe through which
those points of brilliance would pass.

Hillfort

Eddie Gladden grazes sheep now on Rainsborough Camp.
Their cloven hoofprints tread a dance along the rampart wall
and wisps of wool attach to grass in the enclosure.
I climb up from the village through horse-pasture and barley.
The fibres of the seed-heads snag my jeans.
Iron built this camp: not antler-horn or flint. Not bronze
but younger bluer blades: their edges silvering in soil,
the snag of tree-roots, the winnowing of chalk.

A lamb runs bleating at my passage, and the ewes
look up from grazing; stare, retreat.
One squats, squares up and starts to urinate,
her slitted pupils ragged in the eyeballs' gold.
Rain's bergh the Saxons called it – Raven's Camp:
after the bird that perched and whispered wisdom in the ear
of Wednesday's god, the cloaked and hooded stranger,
seeker-after-knowledge, who hung three days upon the World Tree.

Rainsborough Camp. And it was old then.

Eddie clipped the corner of a Villa ploughing an adjoining field:
the legionary's land-right staked within the sight of older settlement,
the *pilum* not the throwing-spear the force behind the claim,
and stabbing-sword and shield-rim to hold it for a while
against the dark. And Wilfred talked of ox-roasts in the fort,
of fetes and games to mark the marriage of the Squire,
the village children fevered and cavorting on the flatland
in their grease-stained Sunday best.

A beech tree guards an earth-fall in the ditch. I duck
beneath the waxiness of leaves, walk the perimeter.
Rabbits warren in the earthworks. I scan their spoil,
hoping for brooch-pins, nails, an arrow-head. Nothing.

Below me, in the place of churls, where the iron plough
turned the headlands of the medieval strips, Pado the smith
makes forty pennies' payment to the manor rolls. And Wilfred saves
each tiny bit of scrap against the day he'll need it on a job.

A car pounds eastwards down the tarmac-scar of Roman road,
turns right for Croughton. Chippings and the loose stuff on the corner
make that noise like packing snow. The engine's revolutions whine,
pistons oiled and eager in the casting of the block.
Then stillness, silence. The faintest taste of the exhaust.
Behind its passage earth resettles imperceptibly.

Lore

And even at its most arcane
the smithing-lore

that we'd call crystallography and
coefficient of expansion

– the way the iron band of the tyre
snugged the wheel-rim,
cooled and bit down hard;

the edge you'd have the chisel keep
whose red-heat you'd dipped
hissing in the bosh –

was knowledge
you'd had from your father.

It worked for you
because it worked for him.

And you committed it to memory –
the secret yours to keep

or pass along
as you saw fit.

Shoes

In the stone at the foot of the cross
the surname "Grant" inscribed three times.
Albert, Arthur, George.
Only one family lost more.
Beneath the roll the lettering:
Brethren Pray For Us.

And does he? I wonder –
the youngest son,
the scraggy lad too young for war.
Is it enough that he does?

He only mentions them once,
says in passing how he misses
the companions of his youth.
As he stepped
into the silence of the Armistice
to post-and-rail the parkland,
shoe the punches and the shires,
to true the plough-blade
and the harrow-tine.

Apprenticed to a man
who'd seen his seed ploughed under
in the soil of France.

And still the farmers in the fattened fields
exhume the bones, the unexploded ordnance.
They prod and poke a discharge: splinters
ripping through the clod.

Unmesh

Seen through a microscope
steel's structure is crystalline:
the grains uneven, interlocked,
each tiny physicality
tangential and intensely taut.

In heat the mesh unclenches,
crystal boundaries blur,
and places that were plated
slide past each other
supple as the zig-zag
on an adder's back.

Dionysos 1

In the throne-room on Olympus
Hera sits.
And sits and sits and sits,
the victim of a joke
of dubious practicality,
and singular inventiveness:
the cause of her distress a chair
which binds her, hand and foot,
a present from her long-lost son,
to whose good grace she cannot rise.
The chair's grip is unshakeable,
its maker otherwise engaged.

I am summoned from my revels.
Admitted to her presence I confess
I'd chortle in my beard
were her temper not so savage.
Flunkeys, bound to silence, swab and groom,
raise dainty morsels to her lips.
The chair reluctantly admits
the intrusions of a bed-pan.

The joke is infantile and wearing thin.
She speaks through gritted teeth:
"Dionysos."
"Madam."
"Fetch my son."

I find him in the forge, dressed up in a cacophony.
He's straightening an axle-shaft.
In his hands it's a twig whirled by a current,
unkinking in the bore of his assault and battery.
His arms are hammer-garlands, a blur
above the stump of his legs.
I watch him at his industry, entranced.
I never knew a god to sweat.

"Hephaistos!"
He puts his hammer down and stows the shaft.
"That's thirsty work, my friend.
Come, drink with me.
I have a proposal to make."

The Trench

1   Strata

We sit in the shade of a hawthorn
beneath a summer's downland sky.
Not a whisper of wind,
the merest stitch of cloud.

Above us, like a blister on the skyline,
the rampart of a hillfort,
in whose shoulder we have scarred
a twenty metre trench.

It's deep as one of us. The chalk
gleams whitely in its bed.
And up the slope the spoil heap piles:
the loose stuff that we've barrowed out of it.

All this week I've watched
the colours of our digging change,
from turf and topsoil
down through shale,
the greys of flint,
to bedrock:
chalk clenched tight with moisture,
a dust bloom filming as it dries.

In the trench's sides
– shaved smooth with shovel-blades –
the strata that we've dug the colours from
lie layered and labelled, numbered:
each one the stage in a chronology.

"This blackening suggests a fire."
"The sarsens from the wall have fallen outwards.

But layers beneath suggest they fell
when infill of the ditch was well-advanced."

And all of this is logical, deductive;
though what's described
lies so far out of reach
we know it only through its aftershock.

We grid the ditch with wire frames,
and pencil-shade its contours
onto cross-hatched draftsman's paper:
the schemata of squares
a smoothing out,
a making-sense – science
harnessed to a storyteller's art.

Each week I go back there.
To the lamplight and the scuffmarks in the carpet,
the steadiness with which
his eyes meet mine.
We lift the covers on the trench
and I climb down.

Some episodes I lift intact,
their outlines easily discernible.
I bring them to the surface whole.
Usually it's shards,
like glints of silver in the screed:
the texture of a nylon sheet,
the broken rhythms of an adult's speech,
the shamefulness with which I sleep
above my mother's protest.

The memories layer in pockets
not of soil, but feeling:
coagulant, reactive.
I trowel round them, pull them clear.
I let what's risen with them
dry and crumb,
wipe at memory's surface with a moistened thumb,
and find it pocked and pitted.

The tears come
with the shock of recognition.
I find I've known each crack,
each fracture
as intimately as I know
my crow's-feet in the mirror,
the marking on my palms,
the faultlines of my heart.

3   *Departure*

We shroud the trench in polythene,
and scumble earth on top.
The spoil sits loosely in the cut.
We tissue over it with turves:
a fissuring of ragged seams.

The faces in the queue for tea
are weary suddenly.
We've sealed up something of ourselves.

The clouds pile over Hackpen Hill.
We stumble in the half-light
of approaching rain. From storm-flaps
we stare out across the site.
Rain needles at its emptiness:
the earthworked contours glisten
smooth, restored.

The canvas of the tent
gives up its scent to dampness.
Goose-bumps form.
And out there, in the storm
the grass-roots in the turf
begin to stretch
and stitch
and knit.

Hephaistos 2

I fell all day,
I fell a lifetime's span.

My final memory:
the grip of her hands on my withered legs
as she swung me to the cliff's edge
and dandled me, dangled me over the drop.
Then nothing —
her hold unloosening and the rush of speed.
Air my cradle and from somewhere
in my guts a mandrake-scream.
My swaddling bands
ripped open in the updraught.

I fell all day.
I fell a lifetime's span.

In the evening,
as the sun's glow sank,
I felt the air about me thicken —
a stink of salt, of richer chemicals.
And hurtling upwards through the gloom
the trace of whitecaps
on the trough of Ocean,
a cup of shadows in the dusk.
Saw — in that split-second
before I struck —
my own extinction mirrored in its surface.
I balled like a bullet, cleft the waters
with a crack that shivered bone;
I splintered to the bottom,
breathless in that fierce deceleration.

Dionysos 2

"She cast me out. She hid her face.
She never loved me, Dionysos."
The catapulting infant in the body of a man.

At the corner of his eyes the waters brim –
a beaker's worth of brine. Even his tears are ugly,
his chin a cleft you could sharpen knives in.
The furnace-in-him gapes, its blaze
intolerable, exposed.
I hide my eyes, reach for the flagon, fill his glass.

There's just one gift I have to give: oblivion.
Sever your soul from the body's shroud
and set it singing, give it wings!
Don't fear to lose it. Just observe
its passage through the world.

Is your misery so important?
Is its value simply that it's yours,
your own thing? Let it go.

"Another glass?" I ask.
"Another!" he says.
His crooked legs grow palsied.
He mumbles, bawls obscenities.
I tell him all the jokes I know;
he laughs. "Another glass?" I ask.

I hoist him, insensible at last,
onto my donkey's back,
examine the bow of her legs with some alarm,
but she's a sturdy beast, and so —
with effort, and with not a little prompting,
we climb, the three of us, up through starlight
to the summit of Olympus.
In the darkness before dawn I slip into the throne room,
ease the burden from my donkey's back,
and prop him in a corner.
I doff my hat and take my leave.

Fire-weld

Sometimes the graft takes
in the instant that you lay the halves
across the anvil's face,
their binding irresistible,
the hammer's pressure necessary
only to displace impurities within the weld –
that mushroom spray of sparks and clinker,
a burst of gritty oxides
in whose stead
the scarfed ends meet and marry,
cleave in an embrace so fierce
its cooling is a fusion.

And all of this the product of a heat
so purely, so intensely white
steel's sense of 'this' and 'that',
of otherness
is utterly confounded.
You watch the coals drink in
the air-blast, yellows
bleaching to a brilliance
in whose glare
the solid ends of steel begin to swim,
grow slippery.

Form slumps.
Distinctions merge.
And if there's magic here, it lies
in your belief
that matter in this state is biddable,
its energies commingled;
the pairing meet and fit and wholly realized
even before the irons
have left the fire.

Starlight

Last night I dreamed I held your hand.
You folded me in the cloak you wore and we stood
on the sand of the seashore staring up at the stars.
In the starlight we turned, we each of us turned
a quarter turn – you to your left and I to my right
and pressing back to back we laid our heads
upon the other's shoulder. Janus-faced we looked up
into night.

       The planets on their orbits pirouette
like shuddering spinning-tops. And the light
from all those distant suns is bent awry
by matter dense beyond imagining.
The stars we constellate are habits of seeing,
but what we saw then we saw as one being.
I saw an ending, and you the beginning.

Love as language

The beach at Hastings.
Shore sea-sculpted out of pebbles –
scooped and lifted, agates and gunmetals –
banked in a curve
between high-water mark
and the sea's breaking.

I remember the shame
of never having had a language to describe
my sense of being buffeted,
the soreness in my heart.

A numbness to it all
because to open to the sense of having loved him
would have been to open to the sense
of having thrown my love away:
the poverty of love's return, the hurt of it.

Which came, of course.
Of course it came.
But my glory, that day on the beach, was to say:
Father, I love you.

Despite your violence and your stillness and your
silences,
Father, I love you.

I can't think of love
without thinking of faith,
the revelation being not that hurt can be avoided
but that, by some extraordinary grace,
it won't annihilate – stands instead
at one extreme of an experience
whose other pole is joy
unbounded, unconfined.
Within that span I glimpse
the scraps of my divinity,
the stirrings of the maker-in-me.
I come to it fresh,
each time the shock of it.

To the shock of sunlight in the mornings,
to coffee in a bowl,
to words won from darkness,
to these words
written on the page.

Granite

You took my heart and split it down the grain.
I woke in the morning to the pain of being doubled,
of knowing myself cleft. All my life I've chased the tale
of being tallow in the flame of my beloved.
So there's shame too in my seeing for the first time
that substance of my being that your heart's exposed.
It's raw and coarse as granite –
which would make of me a villain
were the break not clean, the paired halves
roseate and crystalline, brilliant with refracted light.

Young poem

for Ella

This is a young poem.
The ink behind its ears is still wet
and you can smell
the milk on its breath, the seep of tides
from its severed umbilical.

This poem's down was up
and up was down until just recently
when, with a thrumming heart,
it cavilled out
along a muscled corridor,
plunged into empty space.

This poem lacks for steadiness.
This poem lacks for grace.
Its rhythms are the rhythms of sleep
and waking, the ebb and flow
of milk in the gullet.
It dries out only slowly.

This poem is a Fish, a Calf,
the crying from a Moses basket by the hearth.
This poem came
to unsettle your dreams, saying simply:
care for me.

Letting go

There was a time
when the embers on the hearthstone
crumbled; their worms' glow wisped
and smoke tongued upwards
to the chimney-breast.
There was a time
when the goad was drawn,
when all substance of my injury was spent,
its ashen residue
to be dispersed
not by the fan of bellows
but an act of will – of taking in
and letting out, the gentlest of breaths.

Drawing down

It's the teasing out of stories
from blunt stock.
The refinement of endings.

Take a strand of steel and
heat it till the crystals' mesh unknits;
then compress

the livid end between the downward shock
of hammer-blow,
the counter-force

that is the anvil's weight:
the sheer, unmoving mass of it.
The physics say that softness yields

and elongates.
You feel its stretch through hammer's head
and hammer shaft –

the grain a telegraph to left-side brain,
the left hand knurled upon the stock
to centre and align

the bar beneath the blows.
And steel is sinuous,
not cast as liquid

but dislodged
towards a rearrangement, thinning out.
It's drawn down to a vanish-point

where blows run out on silence,
unsounded, and unnecessary.
The point made.

Samhain

Eight years on from that first letter
I stood by the phone and cradled his voice.
It was All Hallows' Eve and the children next door
had scooped the flesh from a pumpkin
and set it flickering on the gatepost.
We went out picking sloes and when we returned,
bags bulging with the bitter fruit,
they were standing in the twilight
wearing witches' hats, their facepaint
lurid in the lantern's glow.
Afterwards, when we'd pricked the skins
and the gin in the demijohns was purpling,
you asked me how he was. I said:
"He sounded so much older;
he sounded so much frailer than I'd thought…"

Tesserae

On the walls of your workshop
hung mosaics whose tiles
you'd cut from polystyrene sheet and painted –

squares and triangles and diamonds,
their sides scored with a Stanley-knife
so precisely that the meld

they made was seamless:
abstractions, and experiments in symmetry
conjugated out of line and angle – form.

Something within me
rebelled against
the exactness of it all.

It's only now I see
you might have found
the stretch and shade of language

as alien, as threatening
as once I found that interlock:
the play you made of geometry.

Arkengarthdale

In the lee of the pass you suddenly braked
and cut the engine; stood, eyes shaded, staring westwards
out across the ruck of scarp and moorland.
You told me once that you'd felt drawn to study rock
because its weightiness was proof somehow
against the terrors of your childhood. It grounded you.
But what I saw then, mirrored in your face,
was delight in its creation: the world a place of laval force
whose hills before us bunched and gathered
like the folds of skin on a bull's neck,
rippling to the movements of some knobbly colossus,
with rill and rivulet and beck as scoop and gouge to dress
that gritty hide, their courses a gentling just as, then,
the course of your tears refigured your cheeks.

Healing

In my making I myself am made –
as steel bends to the hammer
so I too am wrought –
not by play of force on bone and marrow
but in waking to an essence,
to that self that simply holds the threads
of a story that is known,
is supple in the moment to a choosing:
how this blow falls, and this, and this...
and this caress... and this...

Hephaistos 3

I wake to the knowledge of her gaze,
and weak as the day she saw me last.
All motion in my limbs is a triumph of the spirit
against the giddiness that racks me.
I rise and straighten
in a room that see-saws like a raft.
Her eyes are hagged with sleeplessness.

"Hephaistos."
"Mother."
"May I stand to greet you,
or will you prolong this?"

There's no magic lock, no secret mechanism.
The power that binds her in the chair
is the force of will alone –
I do not will it anymore.
It's too trite: but as the bonds that tie her fall
I find I've set free something in myself.
All my life I wanted her there,
and, now that she is, I do not want it.
Is that love then,
that you cannot compel
its attendance?

I hug the bones of her body, find them brittle,
poorly fleshed, hollow as a bird's.

I lay my head on her shoulder
and find the disproportion of it all grotesque.

"Mother."
"Hephaistos."
Her voice is the sighing of wind in the orchards,
the shout of violets bursting the earth.
I am borne like a boat by a sail
out beyond the sight of land
to a place without bearings.
There is only risk.
And the worst of the risk is not her rage
but my fearfulness of new beginnings.

I notice I am sobbing
and through my tears
I see the god of wine,
his head supported on his donkey's flank,
doubled up with mirth.
His laughter haunts me —
savage, poignant, having for its butt
only a future hanging in the balance.

I offer my mother my hand.
We walk out together on the terrace.

Scroll

is spiralled steel-strand,
is metal snail-shelled in a coil,

is steel
drawn to the thickness of foil,

then furled, the curl pinched in,
and rolled,

wholly,
backwards through the body of the bar

as supple and as darkly sweet
as bootlace liquorice,

as crisp as paper in a roll
whose fibres tension it to spring apart.

So what you wrap is double-scroll,
what you wrap is air;

the solid and the insubstantial
interleave.

But metal's curve
declines, unclenches, trails,

and space confined
spills outwards.

It gathers breath to breast the lip,
the spinning of the tail,

to make of steel a glitch, a hieroglyph,
a comma, not a stop.

Photographs

Acknowledgements

Versions of 'Opening up', 'Tilth', 'Wilfred', 'Gifthorse', 'Dead men', and 'Ammonite' were first published in *Oxford Poets 2004: An Anthology* (Carcanet, ed David Constantine and Bernard O'Donoghue). 'Drawing down' was first published in *Oxford Magazine*, 2004.

'Shoeing shed' was first published in *The Waterlog* (Two Rivers Press, 2001).